T[illegible]ditional Fairy [illegible]ies

S[illegible]d
th[illegible] Dwarfs

Written by Jennifer Zabel
Illustrated by Dorothea King

THERE was once a queen who was as wicked as she was beautiful.

When she was cross, her courtiers cowered in corners and her servants shook in their shoes.

Every day, she stood before her magic mirror and asked:

"Mirror, mirror, on the wall.
Who is the fairest of them all?"

And always the mirror replied:

"You are, fair Queen!"

Then the wicked queen would be well pleased, and for a while, peace would reign throughout the palace.

Now the wicked queen had a step-daughter called Snow White.

When Snow White was very small, the queen had banished her to the top of the tallest tower in the palace, then forgotten all about her.

Many years passed.

One day, as usual, the wicked queen asked her magic mirror:

"Mirror, mirror, on the wall.

Who is the fairest of them all?"

The mirror was silent for a while, then whispered:

"SNOW WHITE!"

The wicked queen flew into a rage.

She summoned her huntsman and ordered him to take Snow White into the forest and kill her.

"Bring me her heart in this silver casket!" she hissed.

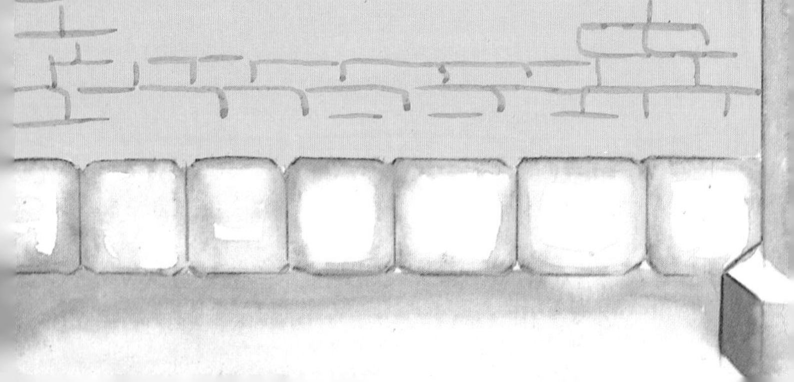

The poor huntsman was too afraid to refuse. But he was a good man.

He led Snow White deep into the forest and took his dagger out of his belt.

"Run away, Snow White!" he urged. "Or the wicked queen will kill both of us!"

Then he killed a deer instead, and laid its heart in the silver casket.

All day long Snow White wandered alone and frightened through the gloomy forest.

Then, as night fell, she came to a crooked little cottage.

When no-one came to the door, Snow White pushed it open and tiptoed inside.

She lit a lantern and stared about her.

"Oh dear!" she exclaimed. "What an untidy little cottage!"

Straightaway, she rolled up her sleeves and set to work on the washing-up.

There were seven bowls, seven spoons, seven mugs and a pan of burnt porridge!

Then she swept the floor and washed the windows.

"Somebody will be hungry after eating burnt porridge for breakfast!" she declared.

So she made some soup and laid the table.

Afterwards, she tripped up the stairs and made the seven little beds and folded the seven little night-shirts.

Then, all of a sudden, she felt so tired that she curled up and fell fast asleep.

But when she woke up and told them her sad story, they straight away invited her to live with them and look after their cottage. Snow White was delighted.

So were the seven dwarfs!

Meanwhile, the huntsman had returned to the palace of the wicked queen.

Seizing the silver casket she rushed to her mirror and cried:

"Mirror, mirror, on the wall.
Who now is the fairest of them all?"

"Snow White, Snow White, Snow White!" echoed the magic mirror.

At this, the wicked queen rose to her feet in a terrible fury, and flung the poor huntsman into her darkest dungeon.

Now, the queen was also a witch. She turned herself into an ugly old hag and set off into the forest in search of Snow White.

Snow White was busy baking bread in the seven dwarfs' cottage.

Suddenly, an ugly old hag peered in at the cottage window, and Snow White nearly jumped out of her skin in fright.

"Buy my apples, sweet shiny apples!" croaked the old hag. "Try one, my pretty, do!"

The apples did indeed look so red and crunchy that Snow White couldn't resist taking one.

But, at the very first bite, she fell to the floor just as if she were dead.

"Well, deary me. How can that be?" cackled the old hag. "The apples are POISONED, my pretty!"

Then she turned herself into a black crow and flew away because the seven dwarfs were coming home.

When they found Snow White, they carried her up the stairs, lit candles around her bed, and watched over her day and night.

At last, they gave up hope of her ever waking up again.

So they made a beautiful glass case to lie her in, and carried her through the forest to a sunny glade.

Sorrowfully, they set her down amidst the flowers, and left her there for the little creatures of the forest to gaze upon.

The summer went by, and the winter.

Then, one bright spring day, a handsome prince came riding through the forest, which belonged to his father, the king.

When he saw Snow White, she looked so lovely and so sad that he lifted the glass lid and tenderly kissed her.

Immediately, Snow White opened her eyes!

Overjoyed, the prince lifted her on to the saddle of his horse and led her away to his father's castle.

Not long afterwards, a royal messenger delivered seven invitations to the crooked little cottage.

Snow White was going to marry the prince!

"Hurray!" cheered the seven dwarfs, jumping for joy.

Far away, the wicked queen watched the wedding in her magic mirror.

She was so angry that she hurled it to the floor, where it shattered into a thousand pieces.

Then she turned into a black snake that slithered away and was never seen again.

The kind huntsman became the king's forester, and was given the crooked little cottage to live in.

As for the seven dwarfs, they went to live in the castle with Snow White, where they never ate burnt porridge again!

Badger Books are published by
Studio Publications (Ipswich) Limited
32 Princes Street, Ipswich IP1 1RJ England

Printed and bound in Great Britain